ALBATROSS

"Navigator's of the Endless Blue"'?

Pragati khadse

BookLeaf Publishing
India | USA | UK

Made with ❤ on the BookLeaf Publishing Platform
www.bookleafpub.in
www.bookleafpub.com

Dedication

To those who seek inspiration and courage in every step of their journey, this book is dedicated to you. May you always find the strength to follow your dream's. Trust me while reading I'll make sure you will smile again.

Preface

"**Albatross: Navigators of the endless blue ?"** In our lives, we often encounter situations where making decisions becomes challenging. This book brings you unique and inspiring stories that offer a fresh perspective. Each page unfolds a new experience, a new lesson, and a new source of inspiration. So, let's embark on this extraordinary journey together and give our lives a new direction!

Acknowledgements

I would like to express my heartfelt gratitude to my parents and especially one of my close friend for their support and encouragement in the creation of this book. Special thanks to my mentors for their invaluable guidance and to my readers for their unwavering support....

ONE

DREAMING

Have You ever dreamed about something crazy stuff? If yes just try to recognise that. I know it will make you smile...

Have you ever seen **Albatross ?** I recognise first time I saw in movie and while I heading to bed I just stair the picture of albatross for few min it's really help me to get some positive vibe's. The best fading dream is while I sleep. I still remember the day I saw the albatross. It was a sunny afternoon, and I was sitting by the shore, feeling the weight of my disability more than ever. Life had been challenging, and I often found myself wondering if I would ever find something that could lift my spirits.

As I looked out over the ocean, a magnificent albatross soared gracefully above the waves. Its wings spread wide, effortlessly gliding through the air. There was something mesmerizing about its flight, a sense of freedom and strength that seemed almost unattainable to me.

In that moment, the albatross became more than just a bird. It became a symbol of hope and inspiration. Despite my limitations, I felt a spark of determination ignite within me. If the albatross could conquer the vast skies, perhaps I could overcome my own challenges and find my own path to freedom.

I watched the albatross for what felt like hours, captivated by its elegance and grace. Each swoop and dive filled me with a sense of wonder and possibility. I began to see my disability not as a barrier, but as a unique part of my journey. The albatross taught me that even with limitations, one could still soar.

The next day, I decided to take the first step toward my own adventure. I began to prepare for a journey that would test my limits and push me beyond my comfort zone. I gathered supplies, researched the best routes, and sought advice from those who had undertaken similar quests. The albatross had given me the courage to believe in myself, and I was determined to honor that gift.

As I packed my bags, I couldn't help but feel a mix of

excitement and apprehension. The road ahead was uncertain, and I knew there would be obstacles to overcome. But with the image of the albatross etched in my mind, I felt ready to face whatever challenges lay ahead. My journey had begun, and I was eager to discover where it would lead.

The first few days were tough. I struggled with the physical demands of the journey, and there were moments when I doubted my ability to continue. But each time I felt like giving up, I thought of the albatross and the sense of freedom it represented. It reminded me that perseverance and resilience could help me overcome any hurdle.

As I traveled further, I encountered new landscapes and met incredible people who shared their own stories of triumph and adversity. Each interaction enriched my experience and reinforced the idea that we all have our own albatrosses—symbols of hope that inspire us to keep moving forward.

Through the highs and lows, I learned to embrace my disability as part of my identity, rather than something that defined me. The journey was not just about reaching a destination, but about discovering my own strength and resilience. The albatross had shown me that true freedom comes from within, and that with determination and courage, we can all find our own way to soar.

TWO

The Journey Begins

With my bags packed and a heart full of hope, I set out early the next morning. The sun was just beginning to rise, casting a golden hue over the landscape. I took a moment to breathe in the fresh morning air, feeling invigorated by the promise of a new adventure.

As I walked along the familiar path by the shore, I couldn't shake the feeling that I was stepping into a new chapter of my life. Each step felt lighter, as if the weight of my disability was slowly lifting. I was determined to embrace every moment, no matter how daunting it might seem.

The first leg of my journey led me through a small

coastal town. The sound of the waves crashing against the rocks was a constant reminder of the vastness of the world around me. I stopped to chat with locals, sharing my story and my newfound inspiration. Their encouragement fueled my determination, and I felt a sense of community that I had longed for.

As I ventured further, the terrain became more challenging. Hills rose steeply, and the path grew narrow. Doubt began to creep in, but I remembered the albatross soaring above the waves. I pushed through the fatigue, reminding myself that every challenge was an opportunity to grow stronger.

With each passing day, I encountered new landscapes and met incredible people. Some shared their own stories of overcoming adversity, while others offered wisdom that resonated deeply within me. I realized that I was not alone; many had faced their own battles and emerged victorious.

As I continued my journey, I felt a transformation taking place. The albatross had not only inspired me to take the first step but had also awakened a sense of purpose within me. I was discovering not just the world around me, but also the strength that lay within. The journey had just begun, and I was ready to embrace whatever came next.

THREE

New Horizons

As I pressed on, the scenery began to change dramatically. The coastal town faded behind me, and I found myself surrounded by lush forests and towering mountains. The air was crisp and invigorating, filling my lungs with energy. Each step felt like a new beginning, and I was eager to see what lay ahead.

One afternoon, while resting by a serene lake, I met a fellow traveler named Mia. She was an artist, capturing the beauty of nature through her vibrant paintings. We quickly struck up a conversation, sharing our stories and dreams. Mia's passion for her art was contagious, and she encouraged me to express my own journey through writing. Inspired by her words, I began to jot down my thoughts and experiences, feeling a sense of liberation with each stroke of the pen.

As days turned into weeks, I found myself growing more confident. The challenges I encountered—steep climbs, unpredictable weather, and moments of doubt—only fueled my determination. I learned to embrace the discomfort, understanding that it was a part of the journey. Just like the albatross, I was learning to soar above the obstacles, finding strength in vulnerability.

One evening, as the sun dipped below the horizon, painting the sky in hues of orange and pink, I gathered with fellow travelers around a campfire. We shared stories, laughter, and dreams under the starlit sky. In that moment, I realized that this journey was not just about reaching a destination; it was about the connections we made and the growth we experienced along the way.

With each passing day, I felt more alive, more in tune with the world around me. The journey was teaching me resilience, compassion, and the importance of embracing every moment. I was no longer just a traveler; I was a storyteller, ready to share my adventures and inspire others to embark on their own journeys. The horizon beckoned, and I was ready to chase it.

FOUR

Unexpected Encounter

As I continued my journey, the path began to wind through dense forests and across rolling hills. Each day brought new surprises and challenges, but I welcomed them all with an open heart. The world felt vast and full of possibilities, and I was eager to explore every corner of it.

One morning, I stumbled upon a small, hidden village nestled in a valley. The villagers were friendly and welcoming, offering me food and shelter. They shared stories of their ancestors and the rich history of the land. I was fascinated by their traditions and the deep connection they had with nature. It was a reminder of the importance of preserving our heritage and respecting the earth.

During my stay in the village, I met an elderly woman named Elara. She was a wise and kind soul, with a wealth of knowledge about the natural world. Elara taught me about the healing properties of various plants and the importance of living in harmony with the environment. Her wisdom left a lasting impression on me, and I felt a deep sense of gratitude for the lessons she imparted.

As I prepared to leave the village, the villagers gathered to bid me farewell. They presented me with a small, handcrafted amulet as a token of their appreciation. It was a symbol of protection and good fortune, and I wore it proudly as I continued on my way. The encounter with the villagers had enriched my journey, reminding me of the beauty of human connection and the power of kindness.

With renewed spirit and a heart full of gratitude, I pressed on, eager to see what other adventures awaited me. The road ahead was uncertain, but I embraced the unpredictability, knowing that each step brought me closer to discovering more about the world and myself.

FIVE

The Mysterious Stranger

The days grew longer as I journeyed further into the unknown. The landscape changed dramatically, from lush forests to barren deserts and towering mountains. Each new environment presented its own set of challenges, but I faced them with determination and curiosity.

One evening, as the sun began to set, I found myself at the edge of a vast desert. The horizon seemed endless, and the heat of the day lingered in the air. I decided to set up camp for the night, knowing that crossing the desert would require careful planning and ample supplies.

As I sat by the fire, a figure appeared in the distance, slowly making their way toward me. At first, I was wary, but as the stranger drew closer, I could see that they were weary and in need of help. I offered them food and water, and they gratefully accepted.

The stranger introduced themselves as Kael, a wanderer who had been traveling for many years. Kael's journey had taken them through countless lands and experiences, and they had a wealth of stories to share. We spent the night exchanging tales of our adventures, finding solace in each other's company.

Kael spoke of a hidden oasis deep within the desert, a place of refuge and beauty. They had been searching for it for years, guided by ancient maps and legends. Intrigued by the possibility of discovering such a place, I decided to join Kael on their quest. Together, we planned our route and prepared for the arduous journey ahead.

The next morning, we set out at dawn, our spirits high and our hearts full of hope. The desert was unforgiving, with scorching days and freezing nights, but we pressed on, driven by the promise of the oasis. Along the way, Kael taught me survival skills and shared their knowledge of the desert's secrets. Our bond grew stronger with each passing day, and I felt a deep sense of camaraderie.

After weeks of relentless travel, we finally reached the hidden oasis. It was a breathtaking sight – a lush, green paradise in the midst of the arid desert. The water was crystal clear, and the air was filled with the scent of blooming flowers. It was a sanctuary, a place of peace and rejuvenation.

Kael and I spent several days at the oasis, replenishing our supplies and soaking in the tranquility. It was a reminder of the resilience of nature and the importance of perseverance. As we prepared to leave, I knew that this experience had changed me, deepening my appreciation for the world's wonders and the strength of the human spirit.

With a renewed sense of purpose, Kael and I parted ways, each continuing our own journeys. The desert had tested our limits, but it had also revealed the beauty of friendship and the power of determination. I set out once more, eager to see what other mysteries and adventures awaited me on the road ahead.

SIX

The Unexpected Encounter

After leaving the oasis, I felt invigorated and ready to face whatever lay ahead. The journey through the desert had taught me valuable lessons about resilience and companionship. However, I soon realized that the challenges were far from over.

As I trekked across the vast dunes, I began to notice signs of life. Small creatures scurried across the sand, and the occasional bird soared overhead. This gave me hope that I was not alone in this harsh environment. However, the sun was relentless, and I had to find shelter to avoid its punishing rays.

One afternoon, while seeking refuge under a rocky

outcrop, I stumbled upon an ancient cave. Curiosity piqued, I decided to explore it. Inside, the cave was cool and dark, with walls adorned with strange symbols and drawings. It was clear that this place held a history, perhaps once serving as a shelter for travelers like myself.

As I examined the markings, I heard a rustling sound behind me. I turned quickly, my heart racing, and was startled to find a group of nomads entering the cave. They looked just as surprised to see me. Their leader, a tall woman with fierce eyes, stepped forward and spoke in a language I didn't understand.

Using gestures, I communicated my peaceful intentions. The nomads were wary at first, but they soon realized I meant no harm. After a few moments, the leader nodded and gestured for me to follow them deeper into the cave.

Inside, I was welcomed into their camp. They shared their food and stories, and I learned about their way of life in the desert. They were skilled survivalists, knowing how to find water and shelter in the most unlikely places. Their knowledge of the land was impressive, and I felt honored to be in their presence.

As the night fell, they invited me to join their fire, and

we shared tales of our travels. I told them about my journey to find the hidden oasis and my encounter with Kael. They listened intently, and I could see the respect in their eyes.

The leader, who introduced herself as Zara, shared a legend about a treasure hidden within the desert, said to bring prosperity to those who find it. Intrigued, I asked if they had ever searched for it. Zara explained that many had tried, but the desert was unpredictable, and many had lost their way.

Inspired by their stories, I decided to join the nomads for a while. They agreed to help me search for the treasure, and together we set out on a new adventure. With their guidance, I felt more confident navigating the treacherous terrain.

The days turned into weeks as we traveled together, facing the challenges of the desert as a united group. I learned to appreciate the beauty of the landscape, the stars shining brightly at night, and the camaraderie that developed among us. In the heart of the desert, I found not only friendship but also a sense of purpose.

As we continued our journey, I realized that the treasure was not just a physical reward but the connections we formed and the experiences we shared along the way. Each day brought new challenges, but with the nomads by my side, I felt ready to face whatever awaited us in the vast expanse of the desert.

SEVEN

The Journey Intensifies

As the days passed, our search for the treasure deepened. The nomads and I traveled through the shifting sands, guided by the stars at night and the sun during the day. Each step we took felt like a step closer to uncovering something extraordinary, yet the desert had its own way of testing our resolve.

One evening, as we gathered around the fire, Zara shared more about the legend of the treasure. It was said to be hidden within the Cave of Echoes, a place few had dared to venture due to its treacherous paths and the strange sounds that echoed from within. The tales spoke of a guardian spirit that protected the treasure, ensuring only the worthy could claim it.

Intrigued, I felt a mix of excitement and apprehension. The thought of facing a guardian spirit was daunting, but the allure of the treasure was too strong to resist. We decided that the next day, we would set out for the Cave of Echoes.

As dawn broke, we packed our supplies and set off, the sun rising behind us. The journey was arduous, with the heat bearing down on us and the sand shifting beneath our feet. However, the camaraderie we had developed kept our spirits high. We sang songs, shared stories, and encouraged one another as we pressed on.

After hours of trekking, we finally spotted the entrance to the Cave of Echoes. The cave loomed before us, dark and mysterious, its mouth wide open as if inviting us in. I felt a shiver run down my spine, but I knew we had come too far to turn back now.

With Zara leading the way, we stepped into the cave. The air was cool and damp, and the sound of dripping water echoed around us. As we ventured deeper, the walls glistened with minerals, reflecting our lanterns' light like stars in the night sky.

Suddenly, we heard a low rumble, and the ground

trembled beneath us. The guardian spirit had awakened. A voice echoed through the cave, asking us why we sought the treasure. I felt a surge of courage and stepped forward, explaining our journey and the bond we had formed along the way.

The spirit listened intently, and after a moment of silence, it spoke again. It told us that the treasure was not just gold or jewels but the wisdom and strength we gained through our journey. Only those who understood the true value of companionship and perseverance could claim the treasure.

With that, the cave began to glow, revealing a chamber filled with shimmering light. In the center lay a chest, not filled with riches but with scrolls containing the knowledge of survival, stories of the desert, and the lessons learned from generations past.

We realized that the real treasure was the experiences we shared and the friendships we forged along the way. As we left the Cave of Echoes, I felt a deep sense of fulfillment. The journey had transformed us, and we were richer in ways we had never imagined.

Together, we emerged from the cave, ready to face

whatever challenges the desert had in store for us next, knowing that we had each other to rely on.

EIGHT

The Revelation

Emerging from the Cave of Echoes, we felt a renewed sense of purpose and camaraderie. The desert, with its vast expanse and endless challenges, seemed less daunting now. As we set up camp for the night, we couldn't help but reflect on the lessons we had learned and the bonds we had strengthened.

The next morning, Zara suggested we visit an ancient oasis known as the Oasis of Truth. Legends spoke of its waters having the power to reveal one's true self and intentions. Intrigued, we decided to make our way there, hoping to find further insights and perhaps more clues about the treasure's deeper meaning.

The journey to the oasis was arduous, but our spirits were high. Along the way, we encountered various desert creatures and marveled at the resilience of life in such a harsh environment. Each encounter added to our understanding and appreciation of the desert's beauty and challenges.

As we approached the oasis, the air grew cooler, and the sound of trickling water reached our ears. The sight of the lush greenery and clear waters was a welcome relief from the relentless sand and heat. We took a moment to rest and replenish ourselves, feeling the rejuvenating effects of the oasis.

Zara led us to a secluded spot by the water and explained the ritual to uncover the truth. We were to drink from the oasis and then gaze into the water's reflection. One by one, we followed the ritual, each of us experiencing a profound moment of self-realization.

When it was my turn, I drank deeply from the oasis and looked into the water. As my reflection stared back at me, I felt a surge of emotions. I saw not just my physical self but the essence of who I was—my strengths, my fears, and my true desires. The experience was both humbling and empowering.

The revelations we each experienced brought us closer together. We shared our insights and encouraged one another to embrace our true selves. The Oasis of Truth had given us a deeper understanding of our purpose and the importance of our journey.

As we prepared to leave the oasis, Zara revealed that the final clue to the treasure's location was hidden within the desert's heart. It required us to trust in ourselves and each other, using the wisdom and strength we had gained along the way.

With renewed determination, we set off once more, ready to face whatever challenges lay ahead. The desert had tested us, taught us, and transformed us. And now, we were ready to uncover the ultimate truth and claim the treasure that awaited us.

Our journey was far from over, but we knew that with each step, we were not just seeking a treasure but also discovering the true value of our experiences and the bonds we had forged.

NINE

The Heart Of Desert

As we ventured deeper into the desert, the landscape began to change. The sands shifted from golden hues to a stark, almost otherworldly white. The air grew still, and an eerie silence enveloped us. It was as if the desert itself was holding its breath, waiting for us to uncover its secrets.

Zara led the way, her eyes scanning the horizon for any signs of the final clue. We followed closely, our senses heightened and our minds focused. The journey had taken its toll on us, but we were more determined than ever to see it through.

After hours of trekking, we came upon a massive dune

that seemed to stretch endlessly into the sky. Zara paused and turned to us, her expression serious. "This is it," she said. "The Heart of the Desert lies beyond this dune. We must climb it to reach our destination."

The climb was grueling. The sand shifted beneath our feet with every step, making progress slow and exhausting. But we pressed on, fueled by the knowledge that we were so close to our goal.

Finally, we reached the summit and gazed down at the scene before us. Nestled in a valley of white sand was a hidden oasis, unlike any we had seen before. The water shimmered with an ethereal glow, and the surrounding vegetation seemed almost luminescent.

At the center of the oasis stood a stone pedestal, and on it rested an intricately carved chest. This was the treasure we had been seeking. We descended the dune with renewed energy, our hearts pounding with anticipation.

As we approached the chest, Zara stepped forward and carefully lifted the lid. Inside, we found not gold or jewels, but a collection of ancient scrolls and artifacts. Zara's eyes widened with recognition. "These are the lost teachings of the Desert Sages," she whispered.

"Knowledge that has been forgotten for centuries."

We each took a scroll and began to read. The wisdom contained within was profound, offering insights into the nature of life, the universe, and our place within it. It was a treasure beyond any material wealth, a gift of understanding and enlightenment.

In that moment, we realized that our journey had been about more than just finding a physical treasure. It had been a quest for knowledge, self-discovery, and growth. The true value of our adventure lay in the lessons we had learned and the bonds we had formed.

As we sat by the oasis, reflecting on our journey, we knew that we had been forever changed. The Heart of the Desert had revealed its secrets to us, and we were ready to carry that wisdom back to the world.

With the scrolls safely in our possession, we began our journey home. The desert, once a place of mystery and challenge, now felt like an old friend. We had faced its trials and emerged stronger, wiser, and more united than ever before.

TEN

The Return Journey

As we made our way back from the oasis, the weight of the scrolls felt lighter than air, filled with the promise of knowledge and discovery. The desert, which had once seemed so vast and intimidating, now felt familiar, almost welcoming.

Zara led us with confidence, her eyes sparkling with excitement as she recounted the teachings we had uncovered. Each scroll contained ancient wisdom that resonated with our experiences, and we couldn't help but share our thoughts and interpretations along the way.

The sun began to set, casting a warm golden hue over

the dunes, and we paused to take in the breathtaking view. It was a moment of reflection, a chance to appreciate how far we had come—not just in distance, but in our understanding of ourselves and each other.

Suddenly, a distant rumble broke the silence, causing us to look at each other with concern. "What was that?" I asked, my heart racing. Zara's expression turned serious as she scanned the horizon. "It might be a sandstorm," she replied. "We need to find shelter quickly."

We hurriedly made our way towards a cluster of rocks that offered some protection from the elements. As we settled in, the winds began to pick up, swirling the sand around us like a living entity. We huddled together, sharing stories and laughter to keep our spirits high while the storm raged outside.

When the storm finally passed, we emerged to find the landscape transformed. The dunes had shifted, creating new patterns and shapes that were both beautiful and surreal. It was a reminder of the ever-changing nature of life and the importance of adaptability.

With renewed determination, we continued our journey back home. The scrolls felt like a beacon of hope, guiding us towards a future filled with possibility. We knew that the knowledge we had gained would not only enrich our lives but also the lives of those around us.

As we reached the edge of the desert, the familiar sights of our village came into view. We were greeted with cheers and warm embraces from our friends and family, who had been anxiously awaiting our return.

With the scrolls in hand, we shared our adventures and the invaluable lessons we had learned. The village buzzed with excitement, and together, we began the next chapter of our lives, ready to share the wisdom of the Desert Sages with the world.

The journey had changed us, but it had also united us, reminding us that the greatest treasure lies not in what we find, but in the connections we forge along the way.

ELEVEN

The Unveiling

The village was abuzz with anticipation as we prepared for the grand unveiling of the scrolls. Word had spread quickly about our discoveries, and everyone was eager to learn from the ancient wisdom we had brought back. Zara took charge, organizing the event with meticulous care, ensuring that every detail was perfect.

As the sun dipped below the horizon, casting a warm glow over the village square, people began to gather. There was an air of excitement and curiosity, a sense that something truly special was about to occur. Torches were lit, their flickering flames adding to the magical atmosphere.

Zara stood at the center of the square, holding the first scroll with reverence. She began to read aloud, her voice clear and strong, carrying the words of the Desert Sages to every corner of the gathering. The teachings resonated deeply with everyone, offering insights into life, nature, and the human spirit.

Each scroll revealed a new layer of understanding, sparking lively discussions and reflections among the villagers. We took turns sharing our interpretations and personal experiences, creating a tapestry of knowledge that was both rich and diverse. It was a moment of collective growth, a celebration of our shared journey.

As the night wore on, we gathered around a large bonfire, the warmth of the flames mirroring the warmth in our hearts. Music filled the air, and we danced under the stars, feeling a profound sense of connection to each other and the world around us. The scrolls had not only enriched our minds but also our spirits, bringing us closer together as a community.

In the days that followed, the teachings of the scrolls became an integral part of our lives. We incorporated their wisdom into our daily routines, finding new ways to live in harmony with nature and each other. The village flourished, becoming a beacon of knowledge and enlightenment for neighboring communities.

The journey to the oasis had been arduous, but it had

also been transformative. We had returned not just with ancient scrolls, but with a renewed sense of purpose and a deeper understanding of ourselves. The desert, once a place of mystery and danger, had become a source of inspiration and growth.

As we looked to the future, we knew that the journey was far from over. The scrolls were just the beginning, a foundation upon which we would continue to build. With open hearts and minds, we embraced the endless possibilities that lay ahead, ready to explore new horizons and uncover even greater truths.

The adventure had changed us in ways we could never have imagined, and as we stood together, united by our shared experiences, we felt a profound gratitude for the journey and the wisdom it had bestowed upon us. The story of the Desert Sages was now a part of our own, a testament to the power of knowledge and the enduring spirit of discovery.

TWELVE

New Dawn

As the first light of dawn broke over the horizon, the village began to stir with a renewed sense of purpose. The teachings from the scrolls had ignited a spark within us, and we were eager to put our newfound wisdom into action. Zara gathered everyone to discuss how we could implement the lessons learned and strengthen our community.

We decided to create small groups focused on different aspects of the teachings. Some would delve into sustainable farming techniques inspired by the scrolls, while others would explore the art of storytelling to preserve our history. The excitement was palpable as we divided into teams, each person eager to contribute their unique skills.

In the following weeks, the village transformed. Fields

once barren began to flourish with crops, as we applied the ancient agricultural practices. The stories shared around the fire took on new life, weaving together our past with our present, creating a rich tapestry of culture and tradition.

As we worked together, bonds deepened, and a sense of unity emerged. The village became a hub of creativity and collaboration, attracting visitors from neighboring areas who were curious about our transformation. We welcomed them with open arms, eager to share our journey and the knowledge we had gained.

Zara took the lead in organizing workshops, inviting experts to teach us new skills and techniques. The village square became a vibrant space for learning, filled with laughter and the exchange of ideas. We celebrated our progress with festivals, honoring the wisdom of the scrolls and the connections we had forged.

However, not all was smooth sailing. Some villagers were resistant to change, clinging to old ways that no longer served us. It became clear that we needed to address these concerns with compassion and understanding. Through open discussions, we listened to their fears and worked together to find common ground.

As we navigated these challenges, we learned the importance of patience and empathy. The journey was not just about implementing new practices but also about fostering a culture of inclusivity and respect. Slowly but surely, even the skeptics began to see the benefits of our efforts. The village had blossomed into a thriving community, filled with hope and possibility. The teachings of the scrolls had not only transformed our way of life but had also strengthened our bonds as a community. We stood at the threshold of a new dawn, ready to embrace whatever came next with open hearts and minds.

THIRTEEN

Gathering Storm

As the village continued to thrive, a sense of unease began to creep in. Whispers of discontent echoed through the streets, and it became clear that not everyone was on board with the changes we had embraced. Some villagers felt threatened by the new ideas and practices, fearing that our traditions were being overshadowed.

Zara noticed the tension and called for a village meeting to address the growing concerns. The atmosphere was charged as people voiced their opinions, some passionately defending the old ways while others championed the new. It was evident that we needed to find a way to bridge the divide and foster understanding among the villagers.

During the meeting, Zara encouraged open dialogue, allowing everyone to share their thoughts without judgment. As stories were exchanged, it became clear that the fear of change stemmed from a deep-rooted attachment to our history. We needed to honor our past while also embracing the potential for growth and innovation.

To ease the tension, we proposed a series of community events that celebrated both our traditions and the new practices we had adopted. These events would serve as a platform for collaboration, allowing villagers to showcase their skills and learn from one another. The idea was met with cautious optimism, and we began to plan the first event.

As we prepared for the gathering, excitement mingled with anxiety. We knew that this was a pivotal moment for our community, and the success of the event could either unite us further or deepen the rifts. We worked diligently, ensuring that every detail was attended to, from the food to the activities.

On the day of the event, the village square was transformed into a vibrant celebration of our culture.

Traditional music filled the air, and the aroma of delicious food wafted through the crowd. As villagers mingled, the barriers between old and new began to dissolve. People shared stories, danced together, and participated in workshops that blended traditional skills with modern techniques.

By the end of the day, it was clear that the event had been a success. Laughter and camaraderie replaced the earlier tension, and many villagers expressed their appreciation for the opportunity to connect with one another. The experience reminded us all of the importance of community and the beauty of diversity within our traditions.

However, as the sun set and the festivities came to a close, a storm brewed on the horizon. Dark clouds gathered, and an ominous wind swept through the village. It served as a reminder that while we had made strides in uniting our community, challenges still lay ahead. We would need to remain vigilant and work together to navigate the storm that was approaching.

FOURTEEN

Storm Unleashed

As the storm clouds loomed overhead, the village braced itself for the impending tempest. The air was thick with tension, and the joyous atmosphere from the previous gathering quickly shifted to one of concern. The villagers were anxious about the approaching storm, both literally and metaphorically.

Zara, determined to keep morale high, organized a meeting to discuss how to prepare for the storm. She emphasized the importance of coming together as a community to face whatever challenges lay ahead. The villagers rallied, sharing resources and expertise to ensure that everyone was safe and accounted for.

As the storm hit, fierce winds and heavy rain battered the village. The sounds of howling winds and crashing thunder echoed through the streets, creating an atmosphere of chaos. Despite the fear that gripped many, the villagers worked tirelessly to secure their homes and help one another. Neighbors banded together, reinforcing roofs and barricading windows, showcasing the strength of our community spirit.

During the height of the storm, a loud crash interrupted the frantic preparations. A large tree fell in the village square, blocking the main road and causing panic among the villagers. Zara quickly took charge, organizing a team to clear the debris and ensure that everyone was safe. Her leadership inspired those around her, and people began to feel a renewed sense of hope amidst the chaos.

As the storm raged on, the villagers shared stories and offered support to one another, creating a sense of camaraderie that had been missing before. This shared experience forged deeper connections among us, reminding everyone of the importance of community in times of crisis.

Finally, as dawn broke, the storm began to subside. The village emerged from the chaos, battered but not broken.

While there was damage to repair, the spirit of the community remained intact. People gathered in the square, assessing the aftermath and helping each other pick up the pieces.

In the wake of the storm, the villagers realized that they had grown stronger together. The challenges they faced had united them in ways they had never imagined. As they began to rebuild, there was a renewed commitment to fostering understanding and collaboration within the community.

FIFTEEN

A New Dawn

In the aftermath of the storm, the village began to assess the damage and plan for recovery. The once chaotic environment gradually transformed into one of cooperation and determination. The villagers, motivated by their shared experiences, worked together to clear debris and repair homes.

Zara took the lead in organizing a community gathering to discuss the next steps. She encouraged everyone to share their ideas and concerns, emphasizing that every voice mattered. This open dialogue fostered a sense of belonging and collaboration, as villagers felt empowered to contribute to the rebuilding efforts.

As they worked side by side, bonds deepened among the villagers. Old grievances were set aside, and a collective spirit emerged. People shared stories of resilience, reminding each other of their strength. This newfound unity became a source of inspiration, as they tackled the challenges ahead with renewed vigor. we see the villagers not only repairing their physical surroundings but also mending emotional wounds. They learned to appreciate the importance of community support and the strength that comes from working together. This transformation marked a significant change in their outlook, as they began to envision a brighter future.

SIXTEEN

The Turning Tide

The focus shifts to the ongoing recovery efforts in the village as the community begins to implement the ideas discussed in the previous chapter. With Zara's leadership, the villagers engage in various projects aimed at rebuilding not just their homes, but also their spirits.

As they work on the community garden, which symbolizes hope and renewal, tensions arise between traditionalists who want to maintain old practices and those who advocate for innovative approaches. This conflict prompts heated discussions, but ultimately leads to a deeper understanding of the importance of blending the old with the new.

we see the villagers sharing their skills and knowledge, fostering a sense of pride in their collective identity. The albatross, a recurring symbol in the narrative, serves as a reminder of the freedom and possibilities that lie ahead. Its presence inspires the villagers to dream bigger and aim higher.the villagers face unexpected challenges, including a sudden change in weather that threatens their progress. However, their newfound unity and resilience shine through as they come together to protect their work and support one another.

SEVENTEEN

Rising Challenges

The village faces new obstacles as they progress in their recovery efforts. Just when the community feels a sense of stability, a series of unforeseen events disrupt their plans. A neighboring village, struggling with its own issues, seeks help from the villagers, leading to a moral dilemma about how much they can give without compromising their own recovery.

Zara, still at the forefront of leadership, calls for a meeting to discuss the situation. She emphasizes the importance of compassion and community, urging everyone to consider the collective good. This sparks a debate among villagers, with some advocating for prioritizing their own needs while others feel a strong sense of duty to assist their neighbors.

As tensions rise, the villagers reflect on their journey and the bonds they've forged. They realise that their strength lies in unity, and this challenge tests their commitment to one another.

EIGHTEEN

A New Alliance

The villagers begin to implement their plan to assist the neighbouring village while ensuring their own recovery remains a priority. As they work together, a sense of camaraderie develops between the two communities, leading to the formation of a new alliance. This partnership brings fresh perspectives and resources, allowing both villages to learn from each other's experiences.

Zara takes the lead in organizing joint projects, including a shared food festival that celebrates their cultures and promotes unity. As they collaborate on this event, the villagers discover common ground and shared values, which helps to strengthen their bonds. The festival becomes a symbol of hope and resilience, showcasing the beauty of diversity and collaboration.

However, not everything goes smoothly. Some villagers express concerns about the sustainability of their efforts, fearing that their own recovery might be compromised. Zara addresses these worries by emphasizing the importance of communication and transparency. She encourages open discussions about their needs and aspirations, fostering an environment where everyone feels heard and valued.

NINETEEN

Unforeseen Consequences

The aftermath of the joint festival begins to unfold, revealing both positive and negative consequences of the alliance between the two villages. While the event was a success and fostered goodwill, it also brought to light underlying tensions that had been simmering beneath the surface.

As the villagers reflect on the festival, some begin to feel that their own needs are being overshadowed by the demands of the neighboring village. This creates a divide, with some villagers advocating for prioritizing their own recovery while others believe in the importance of maintaining the alliance. Zara finds herself in a challenging position as she tries to mediate between the differing viewpoints.

The chapter delves into the personal struggles of key characters, highlighting how the alliance has affected their lives. For instance, one villager, Amir, feels torn between his loyalty to his own community and his desire to help those in need. His internal conflict serves as a representation of the broader challenges faced by the villagers.

As tensions rise, Zara calls for another community meeting to address the concerns. She emphasizes the need for balance and reassures everyone that their own recovery is just as important as helping others. This meeting becomes a pivotal moment for the villagers, allowing them to voice their fears and aspirations openly. the villagers reach a consensus on how to move forward. They agree to establish a system of support that ensures both communities can thrive without sacrificing their individual needs.

TWENTY

New Beginnings

The focus shifts to the implementation of the new support system established by the villagers. The communities work together to create a framework that allows them to share resources and knowledge while ensuring that each village can prioritize its own recovery efforts. This collaboration fosters a renewed sense of purpose and hope among the villagers.

Zara takes on a leadership role in organizing workshops and training sessions that benefit both communities. These sessions cover various skills, from agriculture to crafts, allowing villagers to learn from each other's expertise. The chapter highlights the positive impact of this knowledge exchange, as individuals gain confidence and new abilities that can aid in their recovery.

As the villagers continue to work together, they begin to

form deeper friendships and connections. The chapter explores the personal stories of several characters, showcasing how their lives are intertwined through this alliance. For instance, Amir finds a mentor in a villager from the neighboring community, which helps him reconcile his feelings of loyalty and compassion.

However, the chapter does not shy away from addressing the challenges that still exist. Some villagers remain skeptical about the sustainability of the alliance, fearing that it may lead to dependency. Zara acknowledges these concerns and emphasises the importance of self-sufficiency alongside collaboration. The villagers celebrate their progress with a small gathering, reflecting on how far they've come.

TWENTY ONE

A Hopeful Future

The narrative brings closure to the journey of the villagers as they reflect on their experiences and the transformation of their communities. The hard work and collaboration have paid off, resulting in a stronger bond between the two villages. The support system they established has proven effective, and both communities are beginning to thrive.

Zara, now recognized as a key leader, organizes a celebration to honor the progress they've made together. The event is a joyful occasion, filled with music, dance, and shared stories. Villagers from both communities come together, showcasing their newfound skills and celebrating their achievements. This gathering symbolizes unity and the successful blending of their cultures.

As the festivities continue, the chapter emphasizes the personal growth of several characters. Amir, who once struggled with his loyalties, has found a sense of belonging and purpose. He steps forward to share his story, inspiring others to embrace the changes and challenges they have faced. The chapter highlights the importance of resilience and adaptability in overcoming obstacles.

In the closing moments, Zara delivers a heartfelt speech about the power of community and the importance of maintaining the connections they have forged. She encourages everyone to continue working together, not just for their own benefit but for the greater good of all.

The chapter concludes on a hopeful note, with the villagers looking towards the future with optimism. They have learned valuable lessons about cooperation, empathy, and the strength found in unity. As they embark on this new chapter of their lives, the story leaves readers with a sense of fulfillment and the belief that together, they can overcome anything.

This final chapter beautifully ties up the themes of

growth, collaboration, and the enduring spirit of community.